Copyright © 2021
Michelle Knight. All rights reserved

Softback ISBN: 978-1-737055-42-6
Hardback ISBN: 978-1-956911-02-2

All rights reserved. This book, or parts thereof, may not be reproduced in any form, stored in any retrieval system, or transmitted in any form by any means – electronic, mechanical, photocopy, recording, or otherwise – without permission of the author, except provided by the United States of America copyright law or in the case of brief quotations embodied in critical articles and reviews.

Editor: Sharp Editorial
Cover design & Illustrations: Benedicta Buatsie

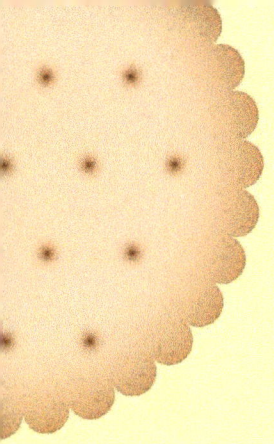

Church, Crackers, & Juice

Shelby Learns About Communion

By Michelle Knight

"Kids, wake up. It's time to get ready for church!" yelled Ms. Jasmine to her children, Shelby and Shelly. "Breakfast will be ready in 15 minutes."

"Mom, will I get crackers and juice this week?" Shelby called from his bedroom in a sleepy tone as he laid in bed.

Ms. Jasmine put her hand on her hip and shouted, "Shelby Jermaine Johnson, if you don't get dressed and come eat breakfast!"

Shelby's sister, Shelly, was laughing while brushing her hair. Shelly was already awake and getting ready for church.

"Mom, I'm dressed and about to eat breakfast," she said, placing her brush on the bathroom counter, still giggling at Shelby.

A few moments later, Shelby joined his mother and sister in the kitchen and began eating breakfast, yet he sat there with a frown on his face.

"Mom," Shelby said in a soft tone, "Why can't I have crackers and juice at church? I'm eight years old. I'm practically a man," he said, deepening his voice.

Ms. Jasmine smiled brightly, trying to hold back her laughter. Shelly, on the other hand, could not hold back and began giggling.

"What's so funny?" Shelby frowned.

"Nothing at all," Ms. Jasmine said, giving her son a warm smile.

As Shelby and Shelly cleaned their plates, eating the last few pieces of their breakfast, Ms. Jasmine began clearing the kitchen table. Ms. Jasmine looked at her watch. "Okay, you guys, we're going to be late for church. Wrap it up, and let's head to the car," she said.

The kids put on their shoes, loaded into the car, and buckled up. Ms. Jasmine turned on gospel music and began humming along with the melody, yet Shelby sat quietly in the backseat with his head hung low.

"Mom, why can't I have crackers and juice?" Shelby asked again as they pulled into the church parking lot.

"Sweetheart, until you are baptized, you cannot participate in communion," explained Ms. Jasmine.

"I asked about the crackers and juice, Mom, not that big word 'camion,'" cried Shelby, mispronouncing the word. Shelly burst into laughter. She was certainly full of giggles.

"Shelby, it's called communion," explained Ms. Jasmine, repeating the word once again, this time more slowly, so that Shelby understood how to say it. "Communion is not a treat the church gives to certain people just because," explained Ms. Jasmine.

"It sure seems like it," Shelby said. "Why is Shelly allowed to have it, and I can't?"

"Mom, please let me answer," Shelly kindly suggested. Before Ms. Jasmine could answer, Shelly began speaking.

"Shelby, I'm allowed to have communion because I've been baptized. Being baptized means you declare yourself a follower of Jesus. It's a way to commit your life to Him."

"I see," Shelby said. "So, can I get baptized today, Mom? Please? Pretty please, so I can get some crackers and juice?" Shelby pleaded.

"No," Ms. Jasmine said sternly. "We're already late. We will talk about this after church. Let's go."

Ms. Jasmine and the kids entered the church and took their seats in a pew near the altar. The pastor led a beautiful service, preaching about the importance of forgiveness and grace. Ms. Jasmine listened intently, and the kids tried their best to listen, too, although Shelby was a bit distracted by the "crackers" and "juice" the pastor was preparing.

Toward the end of the service, Shelby watched his mother and sister eat their cracker, and he wished he could eat a cracker, too.

"I wish I could have a cracker," Shelby muttered under his breath.

The ride home after church was silent. Shelly gazed out of the window, enjoying the peaceful car ride. Meanwhile, Shelby was upset about not having crackers and juice at church, and it was written all over his face.

"Shelby, once we arrive home, please change your clothes and have a seat in the living room with Mommy," Ms. Jasmine instructed.

"Yes, Mommy," Shelby sighed.

As they arrived home, Shelby did as he was told, changed out of his clothes, put on a pair of comfortable pants and a T-shirt, and met his mother in the living room.

"Give Mommy a big hug, and let's talk, grown man," Ms. Jasmine winked while patting the couch, motioning for Shelby to sit.

Peaking from around the corner, Shelly poked her head into the living room, trying to listen to their conversation.

"Shelly, I see you," Ms. Jasmine chuckled.

Shelly smiled and ran upstairs to play with her dolls.

"Son, let's talk about the meaning of crackers and juice," Ms. Jasmine gently said.

"Mommy, I eat crackers and juice all the time at home," he cried, "so why can't I have them in church, too?"

"Well, in church, those aren't regular juice and crackers," explained Ms. Jasmine. "Sweetheart, you are at the age that you should be attending Sunday School. Sunday School is where you can learn all the wonderful things about God and begin to understand the stories in your Bible."

Shelby sighed, resting his chin on his hands. "More school, Mom? I thought we were off from school on Saturday and Sunday."

"Sunday School does not last all day, sweetheart. Sunday School only lasts for two hours," chuckled Ms. Jasmine.

"While I'm in adult church, you will be in children's church, also known as Sunday School, learning the same stories and lessons from the Bible, except your teacher will explain these stories in a way that your age group will understand," Ms. Jasmine explained.

"Mommy, what will I need to learn to get crackers and juice at church?" Shelby excitedly asked.

"You will need to learn the meaning of communion, and I will explain a bit right now. Communion, or as you say, 'crackers and juice,' is a celebration of Jesus and how He gave up His life so that we would be forgiven of our sins and have endless grace and mercy. The crackers represent Jesus' body, and the juice represents His blood."

"Crackers and juice are Jesus' body and blood?" Shelby asked in confusion.

"No, that's not what I said," Ms. Jasmine corrected. "See, this is why you must go to Sunday School. Let's try this again," Ms. Jasmine said, thinking of another way to approach the subject.

"In the Bible, during the last supper with Jesus and His disciples, Jesus took a piece of bread, broke it, and said, 'This is of My body,' and that is why we use crackers at church," explained Ms. Jasmine. "The crackers are not His actual body but a symbol of it."

Shelby listened as his mother continued to explain the meaning of communion. "Then," Ms. Jasmine continued, "Jesus raised His cup and said, 'This is My blood."

"Wait!" Shelby interrupted. "Mommy, were you at the last supper?"

"No, Shelby," she chuckled, amused by her son's question. "Mommy was not there, but I read my Bible, and I know all about this special moment."

"So, if I read my Bible, go to Sunday School, and learn about Jesus, I can have crackers and juice at church?" he asked, trying to sum up the lesson he learned from his mom.

"Well, almost," Ms. Jasmine answered. "You must be baptized first."

"This is a lot of work, Mom," Shelby said, "but I'm ready!"

"Think of it this way – Jesus gave His life for us, so I'd say that reading the Bible and attending Sunday School isn't too much to ask, right?"

"You're right, Mom," Shelby smiled, "but may I at least get some crackers and juice from the kitchen?" he asked.

"Of course," Ms. Jasmine said. "You're still going to Sunday School, though!"

"I know, I know," Shelby smiled, "but I was hoping you forgot already."

"I could never forget," Ms. Jasmine smiled, thinking about the glory of Jesus.

Let's Test Your knowledge

1. Who was the main character?

_____

2. Why was he sad?

_____

_____

_____

3. How old was Shelby?

_____

4. What is the meaning of the crackers in this story?

_____

_____

5. What does Baptism mean?

_____

_____

_____

6. What does the juice symbolize?

_____

7. What is the best part of the book?

_____

_____

8. What happens in communion?

_____

_____

_____

www.ingramcontent.com/pod-product-compliance
Lightning Source LLC
Chambersburg PA
CBHW051300110526
44589CB00025B/2895